Third Edition

Welcome to an educational and entertaining encounter with your RV's "temporary" holding tanks. This *Primer* is explicitly designed to teach you, "What you don't know about your holding tanks!"

Written for all RV enthusiasts, especially those who are:
- Initially "CONSIDERING" RVing,
- Just "BEGINNING" their RVing experience.
- Have been "CAMPING for YEARS," or,
- Living the dream of "FULL-TIMING."

The information within will clearly demonstrate that an RV's sanitation plumbing system is NOT like a house's sanitation plumbing system and give everyone the background to understand why the dreaded bio-waste management "chores" must be conscientiously accomplished each and every time.

Additionally, this *Primer* endeavors to establish a good working knowledge of the black and gray holding tanks that will enable every reader to start thinking in terms of "required sequence of preparation and use," and, thereby, prevent the exasperating, "I DON'T KNOW... IT JUST WON'T DRAIN!" or "OH, WOW! DOES THAT STINK!!"

The included Editorial *Comments* are based on the author's sixty years of experience using and living in RVs (including more than a decade of recent "full-time" RVing) and conducting the business of repairing RVs. Now, he is concentrating on educating the RV owners.

Also included are many tips and tricks on how to help your RV'S "temporary" holding tanks work more efficiently. (Especially the honest answer to tank treatment!)

The ladies are especially encouraged to read everything between this book's covers. Then they will understand just how their RV's "temporary" holding tanks really work, as well as how to safely use and maintain them.

Understanding Your RV's "Holding Tanks"

Bio-Waste Management

- - A Primer - -

by

Dale Lee Sumner

Retired Master Certified RV Service Technician

Third Edition

Copyright © 2021 by Dale Lee Sumner

All rights reserved. No part of this book may be reproduced or transmitted in any form by any means, electronic or mechanical, including photocopying, and audio or video recording, or by any information storage and retrieval system, without permission in writing from the publisher, except in the case of brief quotations embodied in critical reviews or articles.

Published by SUMDALUS-USA
sales.sumdalus-usa@outlook.com

Printed in the United States of America.
ISBN: 978-1-7353063-7-7
Updated: November 2024

Cover Photo – by Author

<u>Other Published RV "Primer" books available from www.sumdalus.com</u>

Understanding Your RV's "SHORE POWER"
120 Volt Electricity

Understanding Your RV's "BATTERY POWER"
12 Volt Electricity

Understanding Your RV's "APPLIANCES"
Refrigerator, Furnace, Water Heater, and Rooftop Air Conditioner

My RV "LOGBOOK"
A Vital Record of My RV's Equipment & Appliance Information

In Memoriam

Mr. Daniel "Dan" Hylle
(1943-2016)

Dan Hylle (pronounced Hi·Lee) introduced me to the need for Hydro Jet cleaning of my RV's holding tanks back in 2007. After he had finished cleaning my Black Tank and had moved the high-pressure hose and nozzle around the inside of my Gray Tank for just a few seconds, I was totally surprised by what came out. The water was coal-black in color! When I remarked, "Wow! What caused that?" Dan just smiled and said, "That, sir, is caused by MOLD! There was a mold colony growing in your gray tank." (I have an allergy to mold and was wondering why I had begun to sneeze so much when I was in my motorhome.) After that eye-opening experience, I've had both of my holding tanks cleaned annually and can honestly say that my tanks are "healthy," and I continue to breathe mold-free! Thank you, Dan! You started me thinking very seriously about the supposedly innocuous holding tank contents that are usually "Out-of-Sight" and "Out-of-Mind!" I shall never forget the many (previously unknown to me) things you taught me about holding tanks. You enhanced my RV knowledge base tremendously. May you rest in peace, my friend. Everyone misses you.

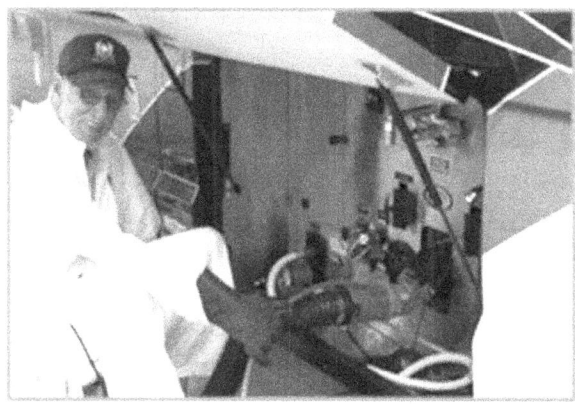

ACKNOWLEDGEMENTS

My special thanks to:

Mrs. Daniel Hylle ("Lori"), Former owner and general manager of Healthy Tanks, RV Tank Cleaning service. Thank you so much for your help and support, Lori.

And, to:

Mr. Don Zimmerman, owner of Tank Techs, a professional RV and boat holding tank cleaning service in Phoenix, AZ, and TankTechsRx.com. Don is responsible for pinpointing the existence of struvite in RV holding tanks. After a persistent two-year telephone campaign, he succeeded in persuading the SCD Probiotics Company to develop a probiotic treatment that would correct the odor, sludge, and struvite problems in RV holding tanks. Following another three years of testing and proving, their combined efforts have resulted in the TankTechsRx product, a 100% natural probiotic treatment. The product label refers to the product as "Totally Green – Totally Clean." To which, I would add, "Totally Keen." Finally, there is a bio-waste treatment product that works specifically in RVs and not the usual chemical throwback from municipal sewage treatment plants or a spin-off of something initially intended for agricultural systems. Thanks, Don.

DISCLAIMER

The text, photos, diagrams, and analogies forming this book are meant to assist you with broad-based, general knowledge and advice toward understanding the holding tank system associated with your Recreational Vehicle (RV). They are not complete, may contain minor errors, and may not apply accurately to your specific situation. They are not to be relied on as guidance for operating or repairing any of your RV's holding tanks or associated components. You are responsible for any hazards you encounter or produce if you "work" on/with your holding tank system. Your legal right to work on some parts of your system may be limited in your State. Contacting a local RV dealership to schedule a "bring it in" appointment or contacting a local, independent RV service technician or professional holding tank cleaning technician to "come to" your RV site are always options and may be required to accomplish necessary repairs or cleaning.

NOTE

Most photographs, images, diagrams, or charts not sourced/credited within this *Primer* were designed and/or produced by the author. The publisher has made every reasonable effort to contact all copyright holders. Any errors that may have occurred are inadvertent. Anyone who, for any reason, has not been contacted is invited to contact the publisher so that a full acknowledgment may be made in subsequent editions of this work.

INTRODUCTION

Webster's dictionary defines a primer (prĭm´ər – rhymes with trimmer) as "a small book covering the fundamentals of a topic."

This "small book" concentrates on the RV bio-waste holding tanks – euphemistically known as the "Black" and the "Gray" Tanks – the parts of the RV that no one wants to deal with. Therefore, they are used and, most typically, abused. To nearly everyone, they're "Out-of-sight" and "Out-of-mind" until something starts to "stink" or starts to backflow out of the tub/shower drain (the lowest drain in any RV).

Additionally, this "small book" was not designed to be a high level, scientifically correct, know-all, or end-all document to satisfy the most critical of bio-waste management engineers, who, in their own right, are operating on a much larger scale of operation and different purpose than the rest of us. It was specifically written to provide the typical RVer (**J.** [*Jane or John*] **Q. Public**) with the basic operating principles of their RV's "temporary" bio-waste holding tanks. This is not intended to be a step-by-step "how-to" book, but rather a "plain language," clarifying book of "**What you don't know about your holding tanks**" and how they should be taken care of. It is designed to educate by explaining to every RVer what the owner's manuals do not.

As a matter of practice, I always start every one of my seminars with this simple but often unrealized fact, *"Ladies and Gentlemen, a Recreational Vehicle (RV) is <u>NOT</u> a house and shouldn't be treated as such!"*

Although many RV owners want to use their motorhome, travel trailer, or 5th wheel trailer as though it was a house, it certainly is not! The interior of an RV may look and feel like a house, but, foremost, the RV can move from place to place while a house cannot.

The RV-specific appliances (refrigerator, furnace, water heater, and air conditioner) resemble house appliances. Still, they are not built the same, nor do they really function the same. (You can read much more about the RV-specific appliances in our *Understanding Your RV's "APPLIANCES"* **Primer**.)

The RV's electrical capability is 50% <u>less</u> (50 Amp) or 85% <u>less</u> (30Amp) than a typical three-bedroom house. (You can read much more about 120 volt power in our *Understanding Your RV's "SHORE POWER" – 120 Volt Electricity* **Primer**.)

Furthermore, let's not overlook the fact that not a single OEM has ever designed and constructed any RV to be lived in, permanently, like a house.

And one last thing, every RV built requires much more maintenance than <u>any</u> house on the market! Yep, that's right, there is no such thing as a maintenance-free RV. That's because RVs aren't designed or built to be a "durable good," as evidenced by the fact that all RVs have a warranty period that is much shorter than the least expensive new car on today's market.

Words to contemplate: Before you venture into the RV lifestyle, ask yourself if you really have the self-sufficient, "pioneer" character necessary to persevere the day-to-day, mundane, and often unpleasant chores that you will be required to do when you occupy an RV (be it for a weekend, a vacation, or full-time). We're talking about chores that, today, are never required or even dreamed of when you live in your comfortable home. Believe me, this slogan is true: "Taking short-cuts to get the chores over with as quickly as possible <u>will</u> come back to "bite" you, later!"

So..., now that you realize that the two "dwellings" are dissimilar and there will be some unaccustomed chores that you will be required to accomplish when dealing with an RV, let's take a closer look at the two different Plumbing Systems and how they affect you.

House's Sanitation Plumbing System
vs.
RV's Sanitation Plumbing System

The House's Sanitation Plumbing System

Once you actually ponder the typically installed whole house sanitation plumbing system for a few moments, the first thing you realize is that it is a perfunctory arrangement that, pretty much, takes care of itself.

It's so easy to operate that even a young child can figure out how to make it work. Moreover, it's very uncomplicated: One merely opens and closes a faucet handle to start and stop water flow at a sink or tub. To fill a sink or tub with water, one inserts a plug into the drain opening or pulls up a stopper lever. To get rid of stored water, one simply pulls the plug out or pushes the stopper lever down. And just as effortlessly, to flush a toilet, all one has to do is push a lever down or push a button in. Could it be more straightforward?

Hardly anyone ever thinks about where the bio-waste and wastewater ever go. "It's gone!" and that's all that matters. Actually, there's a lot more to it. No one seems to give a second thought to the fact that every sink, tub/shower, and toilet (and don't forget the washing machine and dish-washer) drain into a common outgoing pipe that guides all the bio-waste and wastewater from the house into the house owner's septic system or into a city/county sewer system. Quite frankly, this system really *is* "Out-of-Sight/Out-of-mind." Poor little plumbing system, unless it backs up into the house, no one ever gives it a second thought.

Here are some other *Important Things to Consider* about the house plumbing system:

Water enters the house via a single supply line that is tapped into a high-pressure city water system. The operating pressure can be as high as 120 p.s.i. (pounds per square inch).

The house toilet has its own unique 2+ gallon water storage tank. It uses a maximum flush volume of 1.6 gallons to move the bio-waste clear out of the house into the sewage system outside.

And, if you look at the roof, you'll see one or two ventilation stack pipe(s) (as a rule, one for each bathroom) protruding through its surface. They allow any sewer gases to be successfully vented to the atmosphere.

The RV's Sanitation Plumbing System

Whether the RV is self-propelled or towed, the plumbing concept is the same for all practical purposes. The first thing that is different from the house's sanitation plumbing system is the water delivery source. There are two freshwater capabilities in an RV – City Water and Stored Water.

A water supply valve (a bib) is located at almost every RV park/campground site. All you have to do is connect a "potable" water hose between the bib and the City Water Connection fitting at your RV.

(*Comments:*   1. Potable water means safe drinking water. However, drinking water requires a lead-free hose – most are white [or, more recently, blue] in color, and they tend to be somewhat expensive. In contrast, using any cheap [but chemically toxic] "garden" hose is a risky health hazard – don't try to poison yourself.

2. Traditionally, your RV's freshwater plumbing system is rated for a maximum of 60 p.s.i. of pressure to prevent leaks from developing at the connection fittings [elbows, unions, tees, etc.]. Because of the previously mentioned city water pressure possibly being as high as 120 p.s.i., that means you should always use a pressure regulator between the bib and your drinking water hose [not between the hose and the RV – protect your hose as well as the RV's plumbing]. Two commonly sized pressure regulators are available: One is rated for a "Standard Flow" of 40 to 50 p.s.i. The other is rated for a "High Flow" of 50 to 55 p.s.i. If you fail to always, always, always use a pressure regulator, you might as well shoot yourself in the foot – it's that important! [*Remember this:* When it comes to an RV's bio-waste

management, ignorance {or laziness} isn't really bliss – it can be absolutely exasperating!])

An onboard freshwater storage tank (the most common size installed has a 100-gallon capacity) is the second option. This system of stored water requires a 12 VDC pump to distribute the water throughout the RV. Fortunately, the tank and pump use the same freshwater plumbing system as the city water connection. And, yes, the OEM installed a check valve at the city water connection fitting to prevent you from accidentally emptying your freshwater tank to "somewhere" outside the RV when using the pump.

(***Comments:*** **1**. The commonly installed 12 VDC water pump is typically rated at a flow rate of about 2.5 g.p.m. [gallons per minute]. However, because many people want a "powerful" shower just like they experience at home, they replace the standard pump with a higher g.p.m. rating [as high as 5.7 g.p.m. is available]. But, hey, that really doesn't make any sense to me. When you are boondocking [dry camping – no city water connected – the only real reason to operate a water pump], using a 2.5 g.p.m. pump means you can run the pump for about **40** minutes before the tank is empty. On the other hand, using a 5.7 g.p.m. pump means you can <u>only</u> run the pump for **17.5** minutes before the tank is empty. [Hmmmmmm, isn't that interesting!]

Hint: If you boondock and want to ensure the stored water lasts longer, install a 2.0 g.p.m. pump instead. Then you can run the pump for **50** minutes before the tank is empty. And, the pump runs much quieter, too.

2. The conservation of stored water in the shower is another reason an RV isn't like a house. [Maybe you <u>will</u> actually have to learn how to take a "navy" {2 minute} shower and put the concept into practice.])

(*Very important Comment to consider:* Water weighs 8.34 pounds per gallon – consequently, 100 gallons weighs 834 pounds. [Don't forget to figure in the weight of any wastewater in both your holding tanks, too!] Do you really want to use your expensive fuel to move that much extra weight around the country? Your freshwater tank should be empty, and your holding tanks should be nearly empty when traveling [more specific information about this, later]. Just in case you might need water to flush the toilet before reaching the next campground, simply fill a plastic, one [1] gallon jug before hitting the road and place it on the floor next to the toilet. Easy peasy.)

The following differences have to do with the RV toilet. The fact there is no distinctive water storage tank attached to the back of the toilet is quickly noticed. Still, there are several other differences as well. First, how do you flush this thing? There are several methods: a hand-flush lever, a foot-flush pedal, or some electric switch "ON" push buttons. Each of these methods operates one of two types of valve openings – a blade valve that retracts left or right toward either side of the bowl or a ball valve that rotates toward or away from the front of the bowl. Whichever method your toilet uses, the water starts running right away and has to run for at least 48 seconds before the house toilet usage of 1.6 gallons per flush is achieved. (***Remember*** this concept for now. It <u>will</u> come up again.)

Another difference is the non-house reality that the toilet empties directly into a temporary holding tank. In fact, the holding tank (which is usually mounted directly below the toilet) is separate from another holding tank used to collect wastewater from the kitchen and bathroom sinks, as well as the tub/shower. These separate tanks have been euphemistically named the "Black" and "Gray" tanks. Black for the toilet bio-waste and gray for the sink/shower waste. Additionally, like a house, all sink and shower drains have p-traps to prevent sewer gases from entering the RV. Nonetheless, each holding tank is vented separately, through the roof, to the atmosphere.

(***Comment:*** The term "Temporary Holding Tank" means just that. It is a temporary system that is only used until the tanks can be drained [contents transferred] into an approved sewer system [e.g., at a campground or authorized "dump" station]. For some reason, many people believe that an RV's black holding tank is just the same as a house's septic tank. Well, it is certainly NOT! The house's septic system, in reality, is a two-stage, long-term, bio-waste processing plant. The RV's bio-waste tanks are just <u>temporary</u> holding facilities.)

Now that you know some of the differences between the house's sanitation plumbing system and the RV's sanitation plumbing system let's move on to…

"What you <u>don't</u> know about holding tanks."

To begin with —

There are six (6) necessary steps to ensure properly functioning RV bio-waste holding tanks:

1. Prepare
2. Treat
3. Use
4. Drain
5. Rinse
6. Clean

We will investigate each step carefully. But First...

Do You Know the
Real Secret to
Successful RV Bio-Waste
Storage and Disposal?
(a.k.a. <u>A</u> <u>Healthy</u> <u>Holding</u> <u>Tank</u>)

The answer is...

[Courtesy of Mr. Don Zimmerman, tanktechsrx.com]
(Modified by Author)

What's the most common mistake almost everyone commits, whether they are new to the RV lifestyle, been "camping" for years, or are full-timers: They put body waste (a.k.a. bio-waste) into an <u>empty</u> (a.k.a. "dry") holding tank without adequately preparing the tank to receive the waste.

You <u>must,</u> first, add freshwater to "Prepare"

an empty black or gray holding tank!

<u>Never</u> add any waste material to an <u>empty</u> tank, black or gray! To do so will undoubtedly guarantee that foul odors will occur, as well as something much worse. (And, yes, you should add water even before you start dry-camping [a.k.a. boondocking] – RVing without utility hookups.)

How much water should you add? At least "1/4 of the tank's listed capacity." So..., if you have a 40-gallon black tank (and 80% of us do), you must add 10 gallons of freshwater to the tank to "Prepare" it appropriately for use. (Multiply each of your tank capacities by .25 to calculate "1/4 full.")

(*Comment:* Whoa…, don't panic! This 1/4 fill will not consume 1/4th of the tank's volume. This water will, in fact, fill the three (3) inch plumbing line from the tank's outlet all the way down to the termination valves. Only a small portion of the water will cover the bottom of the tank. [The manner in which you can fill the tank with just the proper number of gallons will be revealed later.])

There is another "Prepare" step involved when you "Use" the toilet. Before each use of the toilet, you should always prepare the bowl with water. The recommended bowl fill levels are:

"**1/2** full" when only carrying out the business of "Number 1," and "**3/4** full" when carrying out the business of "Number 2."

By now, you're probably wondering, "Are these bowl pre-fillings really necessary?" Yes, they are! And here's why: Because the RV toilet does not have a storage tank, like a house toilet, that provides the necessary water (1.6 gals) to properly flush away the bio-wastes. These water fill preps will, initially, help suspend any waste solids and toilet paper and then aid them to disappear, quickly and easily, all the way down into the holding tank. The splashing of the flushing water into the tank also provides the necessary infusion of oxygen needed for bio-waste decomposition.

Okay, this happens if you don't "prepare" your black tank with water or "use" enough water. For example, here's one of those images worth a thousand words:

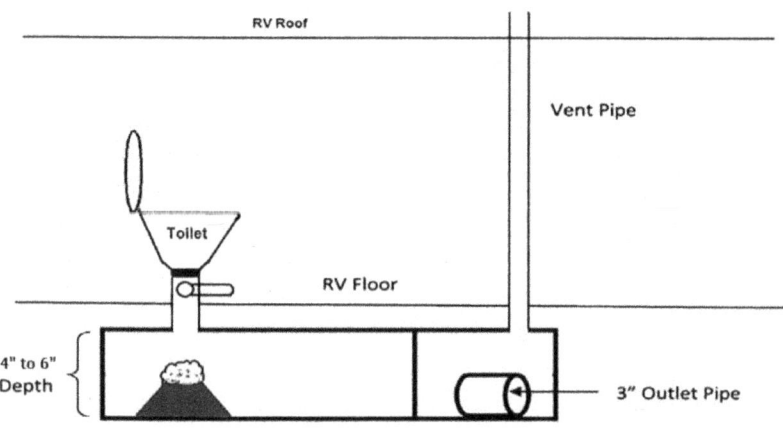

Typical Motorhome or Travel Trailer Holding Tank

The resulting, ever-growing, brown mountain with the white snow cap is professionally referred to as a Pyramid Plug. (How's that for two euphemisms in the same sentence?) Ultimately, it can build up high enough to completely block off the bottom of the drop pipe and prevent any toilet waste from entering the black tank. Oh, YUCK!!

(*Comments:* 1. The holding tanks in most motorhomes and travel trailers are mounted just below the floor level of the RV. Because of this, the depth measurement of RV holding tanks is between four to six inches – most are just five inches deep. Certainly not a lot of depth, but they tend to be long or wide to make up the size necessary for the OEM's designed capacity.

2. Conversely, in most 5th wheels and some larger motorhomes, the Black tank is <u>less</u> than five inches deep. This is because the Black tank is positioned away from the toilet [ahead of or behind, rather than directly below] and, usually, the Black tank is some distance beneath the floor level, too.)

Accordingly, here's an image demonstrating what happens in 5th wheels and some motorhomes if you don't "prepare" your black tank with water or "use" enough water:

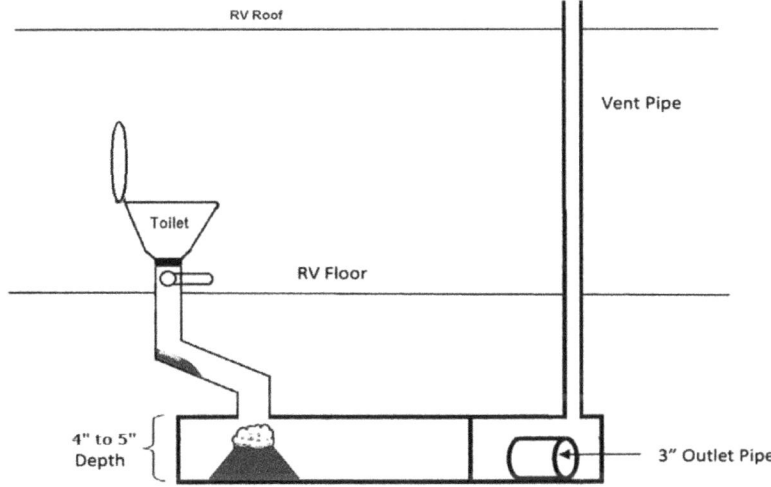

Typical 5th Wheel Holding Tank

The two 45° elbows in the "drop" piping exacerbate an already bad situation. Suppose the bowl is not pre-filled as recommended. In that case, when it's flushed, the limited amount of water flowing out of the toilet into the black tank will reach the bottom of the tank long before the waste solids do. Now you have an even worse problem with a growing brown mountain inside the "drop" piping. And, rather quickly, this additional "growing" problem at the first bend will prevent the toilet waste from draining into the tank. Double YUCK!!

What's your "drop" type?

Okay, so now you want to know which type of "drop" piping you have in your RV. That's easy to establish. First, get a small flashlight to <u>keep</u> in the bathroom. (Good chance you'll need it, again, later. **BTW** – LED flashlights offer more light with less drain on the battery.) Next, stand in front of your toilet. Activate whichever method you must use to open the flushing valve. Keep the valve open. Use the flashlight to see what's below the valve.

You will initially see a large, white, open space below the valve. This is called the "throat" of the toilet. It helps constitute the "height" of the toilet (i.e., how high the top of the bowl is above the floor). Beneath the white part, you will typically see a portion of the black floor flange the toilet is mounted to and, below that, a black pipe heading down toward the tank itself.

It will aid you to see better if the water is running. When the water hits the bottom of the tank or any fluid already in it, it reflects light back up to you. Suppose you can clearly see the bottom of the black tank or the visible surface diameter of the wastewater seems to be the same as the black pipe's diameter. In that case, you have a straight "drop." If you cannot see the bottom or water in the black tank, but just the black piping leading/sloping away from you at an angle, you have the double 45° "drop."

Words of Caution

Besides water, the only items that should be flushed into the black holding tank are:

1. Liquid and Solid Wastes from Your Body,
2. Approved Toilet Tissue, and
3. A Bio-Waste Treatment Product.

NOTHING ELSE!

That certainly means:

> No detergents, bleach, or fabric softeners,
> No ammonia, alcohols, or acetones,
> No automotive antifreeze,
> No flushable or wet wipes,
> No facial tissues, No diapers, No Depends,
> No sanitary feminine products,
> No cigarette butts or cigarette packaging,
> No condoms, No food, No chewing gum,
> No cotton balls, No Q-tips, No dental floss,
> No hair, No cleaning rags, No paper towels,
> No table napkins, No cat litter,
> No plastic bags containing pet bio-waste,
> No grease from cooking, No table scraps,
> And, by all means, no other solids that may cause unnecessary clogging.

Note: The above list is just a sampling of things commonly removed from unhealthy "Black" holding tanks.

REMEMBER: Your toilet is NOT a trash receptacle!!!

Recommendation:

Place a small trash container
(a two [2] gallon size is perfect)
in the bathroom/water closet and use it to
collect the "other" items you may be
accustomed to flushing down the
toilet at home.

Line the container with an appropriately sized plastic bag (grocery store carry-out bags [e.g., Walmart bags] work perfectly) and dispose of the bag and its contents every morning.

Toilet Paper

Which toilet paper should you use with an RV toilet? The initial answer is, "Nothing that is super-soft or "quilted." These types of TP just do not break down in the black holding tank. In fact, they can contribute significantly to a "clog" problem.

So, if you are the curious type, how do you test toilet tissue to ascertain which brand will break down best for you? First, figure out how many brands you want to test and accumulate an equal number of sandwich-sized plastic containers with lids. Fill each container half full with <u>only</u> water. Add one (1) sheet/square of each brand into its own container. Attach the lid. <u>Now the critical step</u> – shake the container "up and down" just <u>once</u>. This will simulate the flushing agitation into the black tank. (*Note:* Any additional agitation/shaking <u>will</u> invalidate the test.) Let the containers sit undisturbed for at least six hours. The tissue that has broken up into the smallest pieces is the winner! Consider that brand as your personally "approved" toilet tissue.

(*Comments:* 1. Beware – a manufacturer "approved," multi-ply toilet paper will obstruct a tank if used in conjunction with chemical treatments. The chemicals cause the adhesive media between multiple toilet paper layers to crystallize and become a clogging agent, which may be extremely difficult to remove.

2. Moderation – many people use <u>**way**</u> too much toilet paper. If you can't cut down your usage, here's a tip to help you figure out which toilet paper should go where:

> If the TP is stained "yellow" – into the container.
> If the TP is stained "brown" – into the toilet.)

Now, let's backpedal a little and talk about Step # 2, "Treating" the bio-waste in the black holding tank.

Oh, my! What to use, what to use???

Ever since holding tanks became a standard addition to RVs, the proverbial question, "What should I use?" has continually haunted all RVers. Unfortunately, the manufacturers of bio-waste treatment products haven't helped the situation. Have you ever wondered why most manufacturers have 2 to 5 different "treatments" in their product line? It's because their "target" marketing strategy dictates they put the same product into different bottles so they can "label" each bottle specifically for what the customer "might" be looking for (e.g., odor control vs. valve lubrication vs. sensor cleaning vs. waste digestion, etc.). That's why it seems like "new" products (made with the same old stuff in different packaging) magically appear on the shelves every year.

You almost get the impression the manufacturers are saying, "Well, if that one wasn't what you were looking for or didn't work, then try this one." Okay…, but at whose expense?

Here's a brief history lesson about bio-waste treatment products:

The original holding tank treatment was Formaldehyde based.

This treatment product is simply a mix of formaldehyde and methanol, along with some blue dye. In point of fact, Formaldehyde delays the breakdown of human waste, just like it does to specimens in glass containers at labs or museums. Methanol is also known as Wood Alcohol. It's added because it has a very agreeable odor that actively masks the hydrogen sulfide (a.k.a. sewer smell). And, the blue dye merely hides the fact that nothing is happening to break down the bio-waste.
Plus, formaldehyde is very toxic. It pollutes the groundwater and cannot be made non-toxic. It is also a known carcinogenic. The manufacturers must know all this because it clearly states on the label:
"Caution – Poison."
For a good reason, this type of product is banned in most places and is not really welcome anywhere.

The Chemical-based holding tank treatments came next.

These types of treatments are based on a wide variety of chemicals. All of them use a deodorant or perfume to mask the offensive odor of hydrogen sulfide. They typically kill off <u>all</u> the bacteria in the holding tank. (Bacteria killers are known as antimicrobial/bacterial pesticides or even biocides).

<u>Common Treatment Chemicals</u>: Benzaldehyde is a simple aromatic aldehyde (smells like almonds) classified as a hazardous substance by the U.S. EPA. Paraformaldehyde is a bacterial pesticide and is a suspected carcinogen. Glutaraldehyde is toxic and is better known as embalming fluid. (Products containing this chemical are usually lemon-scented.)

(***Comment:*** No matter what it starts with if the chemical name ends with "aldehyde," it eventually becomes formaldehyde.)

Bronopol is another antimicrobial that breaks down into formaldehyde. Dowicil is yet another bacterial pesticide that is very toxic to sewer systems. Ammonium Compounds are all bacterial pesticides. Nitrates are nitrogen-oxygen chemical units mainly produced for use as fertilizers. (p.s. Humans are easily subject to nitrate toxicity.)

All the chemicals available typically dilute with each toilet flush, degrade over time, and become less effective the longer they sit in the holding tank. Moreover, the chemicals accelerate the formation of struvite in the tanks. (Struvite will be thoroughly discussed later.)

(***Comment:*** Be very wary of any product that does not list any active ingredients [someone may be hiding something].)

[Courtesy of Mr. Don Zimmerman, tanktechsrx.com]
(Modified by Author)

The "Modern" enzyme-based holding tank treatments

Enzymes are biological molecules (amino acids) that act as catalysts. They are not living things. They are merely a substance that increases the rate of a chemical reaction. They sort of function as nature's "TNT" – they only specialize in breaking waste and nutrients down into small pieces – no other transformation occurs.

Recent U.S. EPA testing has shown that enzymes, indeed, break down the solids. Still, the residue settles to the bottom of the tank as a heavy sludge. Since it is very viscous (sticky) and heavier than water, the sludge makes it very difficult for effective tank rinsing. For this reason, it also prevents macerator systems from operating efficiently. Why? Because the surfactant contained in the treatment solution causes the water to simply flow over the sludge instead of moving it (i.e., no surface tension). (See Addendum # 3, page 76.)

[Courtesy of Mr. Don Zimmerman, tanktechsrx.com]
(Modified by Author)

What's wrong with all these "efforts" to produce an effective holding tank treatment? Well, even to the most casual of observers, it must undoubtedly seem like every treatment manufacturer is still trying to solve an age-old problem with antiquated and obsolete logic.

What is this problem that has been around for centuries?

It's the ineffective breakdown of our body waste and the associated "STINK."

But now, there's a New Approach to solving the exasperating Ancient Problem:

Task-Specific Bacteria

They've been around for over three billion years. And not surprisingly, there are "good" and "bad" bacteria. The "bad" ones (disease carriers) can obviously hurt us, but the "good" bacteria are essential to us because they are very task-specific. The ones we want to use are known as "decomposers." They eat biological waste products and process them down more efficiently and completely.

"Decomposers" are a mixture of
Good Bacteria – Neutral Bacteria – Bad Bacteria

Interestingly, 90% of the "decomposer" bacteria are neutral in nature. Another term for them is Bi-Functional. That simply means they can use oxygen when it is present or live without it when it is not.

A small percentage (5%) of the "decomposers" are considered to be "good" bacteria. And conversely, the other small percentage (5%) are considered "bad" bacteria.

Most dictionaries cite a standard definition of a **quorum** as "the minimum number of members of a group necessary to conduct the business of that group." Therefore, we need a quorum of beneficial bacteria to get biology working for us in our holding tank. To acquire this quorum, we need the small percentage of the "good" bacteria to be the MOST prolific. To help them do so, they need to "talk" to the neutral bacteria and persuade them to act just like "good" guys.

(***Comment:*** According to new research discoveries, all bacteria communicate via "chemical" words – both intraspecies and interspecies. Here's a link to the video. Type it into your browser's search line:

http://www.ted.com/talks/bonnie_bassler_on_how_bacteria_ talk?subtitle=en [there are no spaces]

or,
You could merely search for: Bonnie Bassler ted talk)

The Quorum of "Decomposer" Bacteria can function One of Two Ways:

Anaerobically
or
Aerobically

Anaerobically means that they do <u>not</u> require oxygen to exist and multiply. These are the unwanted, "bad" bacteria.

Aerobically means that they require oxygen to survive and thrive. These are our "good" bacteria. They use the infused oxygen in the water.

Interestingly enough, there is a difference in the size of the two types of bacteria, too. Aerobic bacteria (the "good" guys) are fifty (50) times larger than anaerobic bacteria. As a result, they are much more efficient at consuming organic waste. So, not very surprisingly, we want these guys on our side.

One characteristic of both bacteria is that they make copies of themselves using a reproductive process called *Binary Fission*. This simply means they split in half and make two identical copies – both with the same structure, genetic information, and capabilities of the original cell.

And they can multiply amazingly fast.

As fast as once every 20 minutes!

Start with one (1) bacterium at 9 am on any day

by noon you will have 512,
by 4 pm, you will have over 2 million, and
by 8 pm, you will have nearly 9 thousand million!

All in less than 12 hours!!!

The "Bad" Guys

(Acid & Methane Formers)

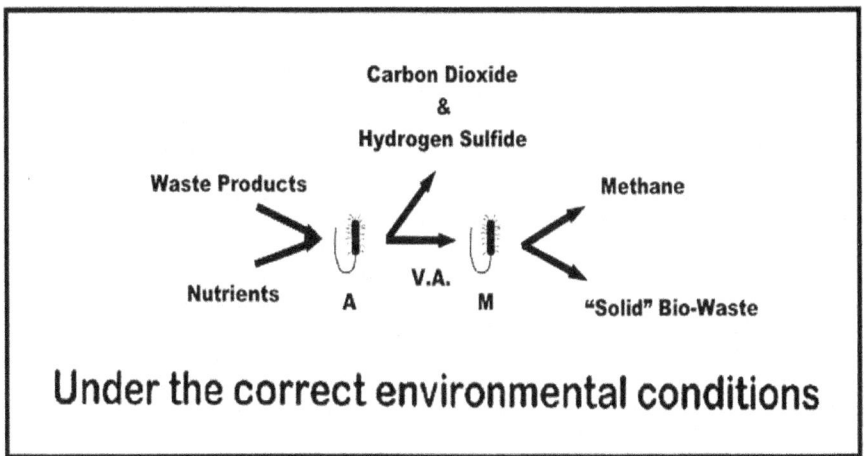

Under the correct environmental conditions

Quite startlingly, if a black holding tank sits for only a day and a half without any (or little) water, it will promptly become anaerobic. This happens because the "bad" bacteria (which don't need oxygen to survive and thrive) become prolific and established control over the quorum.

These holding tank acid formers (A) ingest human waste products and other nutrients and expel carbon dioxide, hydrogen sulfide, and volatile acids. <u>The hydrogen sulfide gas they expel is the obnoxiously odorous sewer gas</u> (i.e., the foul, rotten egg smell)!

The volatile acids (V.A.), also known as organic acids, are ingested by other anaerobic bacteria called methane formers (M). Fortunately, the methane gas they expel has no odor; however, their bio-waste is very dense and viscous. Put another way, they create "sinkers."

The "Good" Guys

(Bio-Waste Digesters)

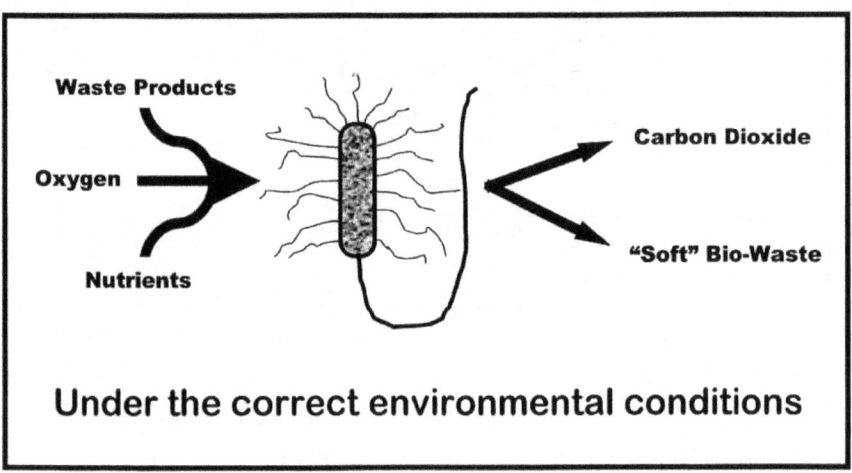

Our friends, the aerobic bacteria, survive and thrive as they ingest oxygen, human waste products, and other "nutrients" from their environment and thoroughly process everything. They only expel carbon dioxide gas (no odor) and their own waste product. Their bio-waste is stable but uniquely soft and porous in form (kind of like a sponge). Put another way, they create "floaters."

Aerobic bacteria exist naturally in nature, but your RV's black holding tank is not natural. This means that something besides water must be added to the system to get things working properly. Enter the new rising star!

A 100% natural probiotic tank treatment will add beneficial aerobic bacteria to your tank! And, as you would expect, the added aerobic bacteria will multiply to accommodate any tank size!

There is, in fact, a probiotic tank treatment that has been specifically designed for RV holding tanks. Its brand name is **TankTechsRx**. It is not the usual chemical throwback from municipal sewage treatment plants or a spin-off of something initially intended for agricultural systems. Instead, it was uniquely developed by TankTechsRx.com, in partnership with SCD Probiotics, and is available in 34 oz. and 16 oz bottles.

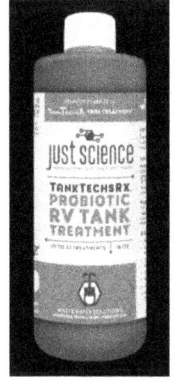

[Courtesy of JustScience.com]

Holding Tank Management with TankTechsRx

TankTechsRx is a "first of its kind," 100% natural probiotic for use as an RV holding tank treatment. A prescribed dosage consists of adding only one-half (1/2) ounce (that's 3 teaspoons or 1 tablespoon – or, if you're using the liter bottle, almost two caps-full) of TankTechsRx into a holding tank (Black via the toilet or Gray via a sink) and a sufficient quantity of freshwater to get things functioning correctly (see pages 16-17).

TankTechsRx is totally organic and safe for use without worrying about the need for critical first aid actions if you inadvertently ingest some or splash any on your skin or in your eyes. TankTechsRx is also 100% biodegradable and, therefore, 100% environmentally safe. It will not harm any bio-waste treatment system (personal or community).

TankTechsRx comes with only ONE (1) CAUTION: Do NOT add any other tank treatment product(s) or any commercial/ homemade cleaning product(s) to your holding tank(s) when using TankTechsRx. That's because TankTechsRx is made up of live, aerobic microorganisms that are susceptible to any biocides (e.g., anti-bacterial, harsh chemicals, bleach, etc.). Instead, we recommend using a spray bottle filled with full-strength, distilled, white vinegar and paper towels to clean your RV's sinks, showers, tubs, and toilets (see Addendum # 1, page 74).

TankTechsRx provides an odor-free and mold-free holding tank environment, positive bio-waste decomposition, efficient tank draining, reduced struvite build-up, and pro-active tank cleansing when your RV is in storage.

A Probiotic is unique in different ways:
[Courtesy of Mr. Don Zimmerman, tanktechsrx.com]

1. "**Eliminates Odor** – no need for deodorants or perfumes. Any odor-causing anaerobic quorum is quickly superseded."

2. "**Cleans Sensors** – and keeps them clean."

3. "**Survives Heat** – continues working and reproducing, even in high temperatures."

4. "**Improves Rinsing System/Macerator Function** – "Floaters" drain out quickly. Other products promote anaerobic bio-waste (heavy sludge)."

5. **Cleans Tanks During Storage** – Aerobic bacteria continue to "work" and multiply until drained from the tank.

6. "**Creates a Healthy Environment** – disease causing bacteria "die," and healthful antioxidants are produced."

7. "**Actually Works While Traveling** – "Drain" both holding tanks, first. Then, "Prepare" and "Treat" with a probiotic in each tank before hitting the road. The probiotic will start "working" for you right away. It will also stop any tank odor from coming into the RV during travel." (See Addendum # 6, page 80.)

What's that you said? You just realized that "Water, Water, Water, and a Probiotic Tank Treatment constitute the "One-Two Combination" necessary to truly ensure a healthy holding tank."

Congratulations! That's called an "AH HA!!!" moment.

But, please remember, keeping a healthy holding tank is a delicate balancing act. There are some other factors to worry about as well.

So..., here's another secret about maintaining your holding tanks:

Holding Tanks, especially the Black Tank, should <u>NOT</u> be drained until the tank is <u>at least</u> three quarters (3/4's) full.

Admittedly, this secret is not genuinely self-explanatory, but demonstrated below is the reason it is so important.

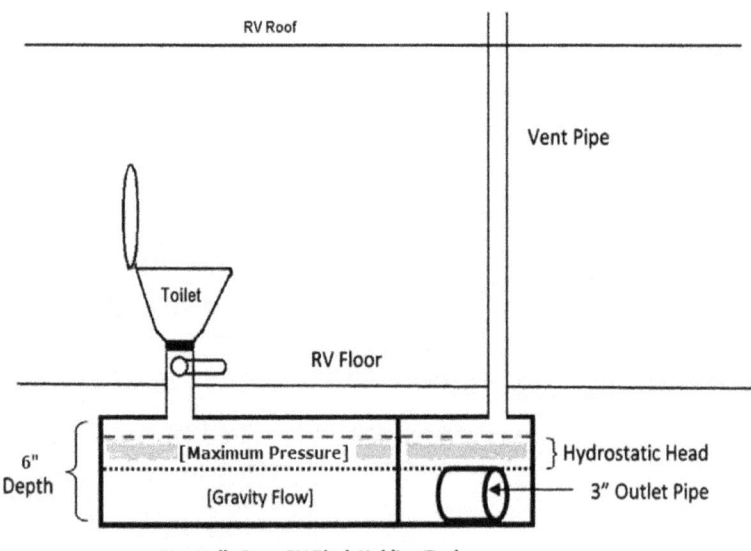

Atypically Deep RV Black Holding Tank

Any "3/4 full" black holding tank can easily be divided into three separate functional areas. For example, let's say your tank is an unusual six inches deep. **1.** The bottom three inches equals the height of the 3" outlet pipe fitted to the tank. **2.** The almost two inches above that is the location of something referred to as a necessary Hydrostatic Head. **3.** The top inch or so is your safe area to ensure you don't overfill the tank.

The hydrostatic head is established because of the weight of the water in this area. This weight will provide the pressure needed to force a good portion of the suspended waste solids out of the tank. With hydrostatic pressure (that's physics working for us), the fluid and waste material movement is quite fast and relatively quiet – all you hear is the soft sound of water passage.

However, the hydrostatic head is expended as soon as the water level breaches the top of the 3" outlet pipe. And, once the hydrostatic pressure is dissipated, gravity is the only force acting on the remaining water and waste solids in the tank. Gravity flow is relatively slow and noisy – air is entering the tank via the sewer hose, causing loud gurgling and splashing sounds.

(***Comments:*** **1.** A law of physics clearly states that gravity <u>cannot</u> push water uphill. So, suppose your RV is on a grade sloping in the opposite direction of your termination valves. In that case, not everything in the black tank is going to drain out. [Hmmm, maybe you can do something about that with leveling jacks or stabilizing jacks.]

2. And, speaking of gravity, contrary to popular belief, a macerator system merely relies on hydrostatic pressure and/or gravity flow to "feed" its input side. A macerator doesn't suck anything; it only pumps on the outlet side. In other words, it does nothing special to drain your holding tank; it just operates like your garbage disposal at home – but it does have some capability of pumping, somewhat, "uphill" if needed.

3. If you leave the "black" valve open all the time, the tank will constantly drain the liquid off and leave the "black" bio-waste behind. The inevitable, but guaranteed, result: You <u>will</u> create a brown mountain with a white snow cap inside the tank [see pages 18 & 19]. And, when the mountain dries out, it's as hard as concrete!)

Before we discuss the secrets about draining your holding tanks, let's first talk about a significant "rule-of-thumb" that is meant to help you safeguard your personal health:

You are <u>only</u> ready to empty your RV Holding Tanks, <u>when</u> you have the right tools on hand.

First and Foremost

1. Use Disposable gloves. Yes, if you aren't one already, you need to become a germophobe.

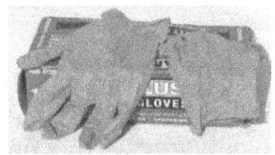

Disposable gloves may be purchased at any drug store, grocery store, superstore, etc.

(*Comment:* Always wear disposable gloves (non-sterile are just fine) whenever you are dealing with ANY part[s] of the bio-waste draining system – for **ANY** reason!!! [BTW – the loose-fitting, flimsy, vinyl food service gloves don't work too well.])

2. If you have an installed holding tank rinsing (a.k.a. flushing) system, you need to **use a separate Rinse Hose**!

<u>CARDINAL RULE</u>: **Never, never, never** use your freshwater hose to rinse a holding tank <u>or</u> sewer hose!!

Recommendation: Always utilize a <u>gray</u>-colored hose to ensure the correct hose is attached to the rinse system every time.

(*Comment:* Here's a twofold "Bad Example" that I witness at RV campgrounds and "dump" stations, far more often than I should!

[No Gloves & Rinsing the Sewer Hose with a Freshwater Hose])

Friendly advice: Don't <u>ever</u> let your fellow RVers catch you doing this! Trust me – they'll never, again, shake hands with you!

3. Use a see-through hose adapter to verify your tanks have finished emptying and the rinse water is clean/clear.

[Courtesy of lightningrv.com]

See-through adapters come in 45°, 90°, and 180° shapes. Use whichever adapter is best for your connection.

4. Use Sewer Extension Hoses, Drip Caps, <u>and</u> a Support System.

with   and

[Courtesy of lightningrv.com]

Extension hoses are available in 5 ft. and 10 ft. lengths. They can easily be attached to one another to extend the hose length. The drip caps are also beneficial when storing the hoses – 1 set for each extension.

(*Comments:* **a.** Two 5 ft. and two 10 ft. extensions are best. With these four extensions, you can configure 6 different combinations from 5 ft. to 30 ft. [5', 5'+5', 5'+10', 10'+10', 5'+10'+10', & 5'+5'+10'+10']. Only use the combination you need – no excuse for any excess hose snaking all over the ground, filling up with bio-waste and water, and sitting in the sun all day! (Um, Yuck.)

b. A sewer hose support system will provide an off-the-ground, downward slope that will allow the hose to drain efficiently, preventing it from remaining chock-full of bio-waste and wastewater that must be drained manually. Consider a versatile 30 ft., expandable support that collapses to an easy-to-store size.)

5. Use a "Drop" Adapter (90° w/bayonet fitting) **and a Sponge Ring.**

and

[Courtesy of lightningrv.com]

The adapter and sponge ring will ensure a tight, leak-proof fit to almost all sewer systems. (*Note:* The sponge ring (a.k.a. Donut) is required by law in many states – Florida, for sure!)

By the way...just so you know –

This type of sewer connection is UNLAWFUL in all States.

<u>NEVER</u> use an open-ended sewer hose to drain your holding tanks! The bio-waste material is too likely to spill out onto the ground (and possibly you). Another problem – the hose can be sucked into the sewer piping, tear off, and literally jam up the underground plumbing system. (Then, you'll have the campground owner really mad at you!)

6. **Use bleach wipes or a spray bottle of bleach** for sanitizing fittings.

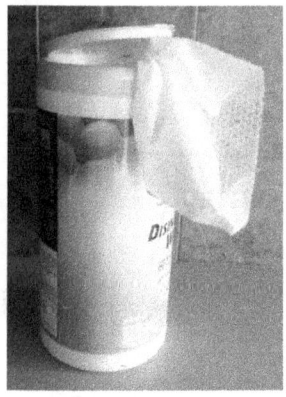 or

Use bleach wipes or spray to sanitize ALL bio-waste system connections – after using / before storing.

And, Last, but <u>not</u> <u>Least</u>

7. **Use a hand sanitizer** to clean up your hands after removing your disposable gloves.

Suppose you need to dry your hands after using a hand sanitizer. In that case, you should <u>only</u> use paper towels and dispose of them properly, too.

These gloves are <u>NOT</u> acceptable for working with RV holding tanks!

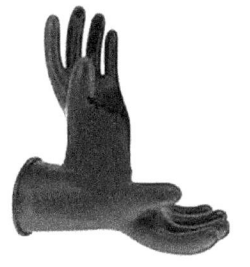 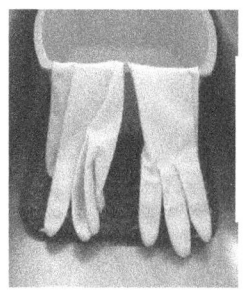

Rubber Gloves

(Electrician or Household)

or

And CERTAINLY not

Leather Gloves

(Any type)

Rubber gloves and leather gloves are just germ incubators! The most common and dangerous germs found on, near, or in the bio-waste draining system and equipment are E. coli and the Hepatitis Viruses.

After you remove these disgusting germ factories – or you don't use gloves at all – and, while you are traveling, you drain your holding tanks every morning before hitting the road, what's the next thing you touch for an extended period of time?

THIS!!

Repeated and extended exposure to E. coli and Hepatitis Viruses just isn't worth the health risk!

(***Study Case:*** Let's say a group of RVers are on an extended road trip together and do drain their holding tanks each morning. Then, following a full day of traveling, one of the drivers has abdominal cramps, vomiting, and diarrhea shortly after their evening meal. Most people would probably assume it was just a touch of food poisoning from the restaurant, where they had just eaten dinner. But, suppose that driver was the only one in the travel group who got sick!

Well, here's an interesting fact: Food poisoning doesn't usually affect us until 6 to 24 hours <u>after</u> we've eaten contaminated food – not right away. This is because it takes time for the microscopic "bad" bacteria to multiply into a large enough quorum to cause a human (the larger organism) to really feel disagreeable discomfort or harm.

Hmmmmm…, sort of makes you wonder, doesn't it? What might that driver have been doing, possibly unsafely, six hours or more hours before the "sudden" discomfort???)

Draining the Holding Tanks
(a.k.a. "Dumping")

Make sure the "Gray" Valve is <u>CLOSED</u> **before** you open the "Black" Valve.

NEVER have both valves open at the same time! If they are, you <u>will</u> cause cross-contamination between the tanks, resulting in significantly bad smells inside the RV <u>and</u> worse.

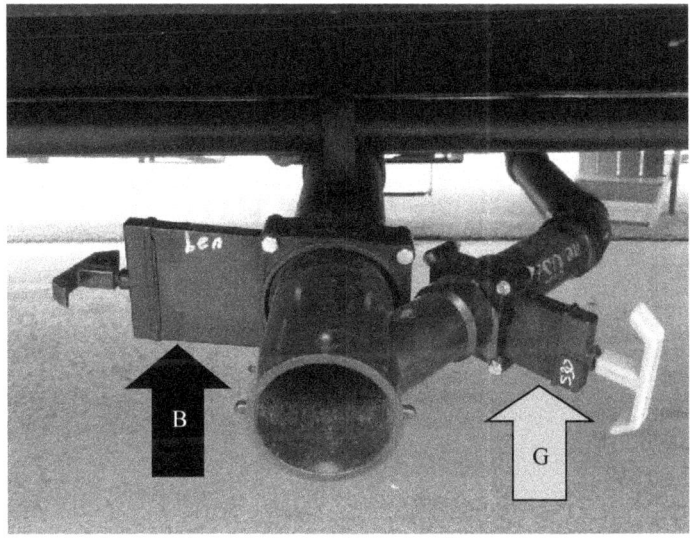

To avoid confusion, the "black" tank's drain line and termination valve are typically larger than the gray tank's line and valve [(B) **3"** vs. **1-1/2"** (G)]. Sometimes the "gray" valve handle is, in reality, gray in color.

And the old adage still applies – "By draining the "black" tank first and the "gray" tank second, the "gray" water will rinse out the sewer hose." (See Addendum # 4, page 78 for Step-by-Step Information.)

A Significant Problem Affecting Drainage
(This one is very prevalent in 5th wheels and travel trailers.)

As mentioned before, most holding tanks are not very deep, but they tend to be very long or wide – sometimes as long or wide as the undercarriage of the RV. On 5th wheels and/or travel trailers that don't have an enclosing cover (called a belly pan) over the undercarriage, you can see the exposed tank(s) if you lie on the ground and look under the RV.

If your tank bottoms are exposed, take a close look at how the tank(s) are mounted. The vast majority of holding tanks in trailers are not supported across the bottom in any significant manner. Because of this, they tend to develop a sagging underbelly as they fill up. The level of this belly actually drops below the bottom of the 3" outlet pipe. I'm sure you get the idea that a tank with a belly will not drain completely. (**Remember:** Water does not flow uphill!)

So..., do you have a belly problem or not? Here is an easy way to determine if your tank(s) have a sagging belly (even if you have a belly pan): If the RV is "level" and the draining tank stops flowing somewhat abruptly, it has a flat bottom. If the draining tank's liquid dribbles out for 5 to 15 minutes after the main draining is done, it most likely has a sagging belly.

The slow dribbling results from the plastic's memory slowly returning the tank bottom to its original shape (i.e., flat) after the weight of the collected water has been removed. If the tank is old and doesn't "lose" its belly, the belly is, obviously, permanent. Unfortunately, this is the case for 90% of the older RVs still in service. A permanent sagging belly is the likely reason the "1/4th or 1/3rd full" level sensor may not go out or goes out slowly. (See..., a bulging belly isn't good for you.)

Something Unique About Fifth Wheels

Many fifth-wheel trailers have something most other RVs do not have – a separate galley holding tank. (This is quite common for 5th wheel units with the kitchen in the rear.) It is a third holding tank. That means there is one black tank, a gray tank for the bathroom sink and tub/shower, and a gray tank for the sink in the kitchen.

And, it may come as a big surprise to find out the two gray tanks are <u>not</u> plumbed together! Unfortunately, many a "first-time" fifth wheel owner didn't realize there was a separate tank for the galley until the wastewater started backing up into the kitchen sink. Oops!

The termination valve for this third tank is usually on the frame wall near/between the tires or in the rear of the unit. To prevent the additional difficulty of moving the sewer drain hose from one drain connection to another, several enterprising manufacturers have developed a sewer wye similar to the water wye for the bib (but no shut-off valves in the sewer wye). Here's just one way the system could be set up:

Source: forestriverforums.com]

Rinsing the Black Tank
(a.k.a. "Flushing")

Black Tank Rinsing is best accomplished one of two ways:

1. By back-flooding via an installed Black Tank Flush (Rising) System.

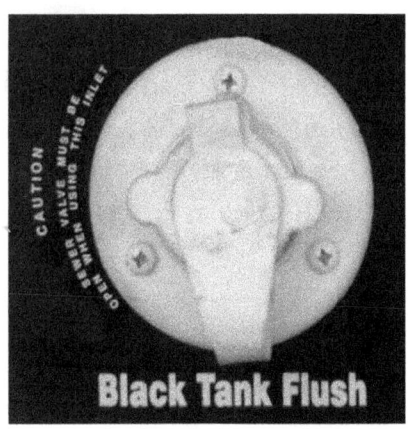

2. By back-flooding via the toilet with a Johnny Chock.

WARNING!! Both methods are considered to be risky – especially if you are not alert. "Attention-to-detail" is a mandatory requirement while executing either of these methods. Failure to pay close attention may easily result in flooding the interior of your RV with "black" water and bio-waste.

Method #1: The Black Tank Rinsing System

Note: This method is only applicable if your RV has an installed Black Tank Flush (a.k.a. Rinsing) System. OEM systems are the norm. On the other hand, several third-party kits are available for aftermarket installation (if you can get to the tank[s]).

Unfortunately, these "flush" systems are not as efficient as they seem. They actually provide the user with a false sense of security or accomplishment. Because of the way they inherently operate, they cannot be 100% effective. This means it is absolutely impossible to rinse out all of the bio-waste left in the tank after the draining procedure has finished using this system alone. When operating this system according to the OEM's instructions, what you actually accomplish is some sort of rinse only in the direct path of the rinsing nozzle.

Why? Well, first, let's look at the tank itself. Unless you were present when the OEM installed the holding tanks in your RV, you most likely have no idea how they are shaped or actually plumbed. Holding tanks come in many sizes and shapes – sometimes with steps, bump-outs, drops, L's, and other geometric contortions.

Here's a diagram of just one of many unusual black tank configurations I've come across over the years:

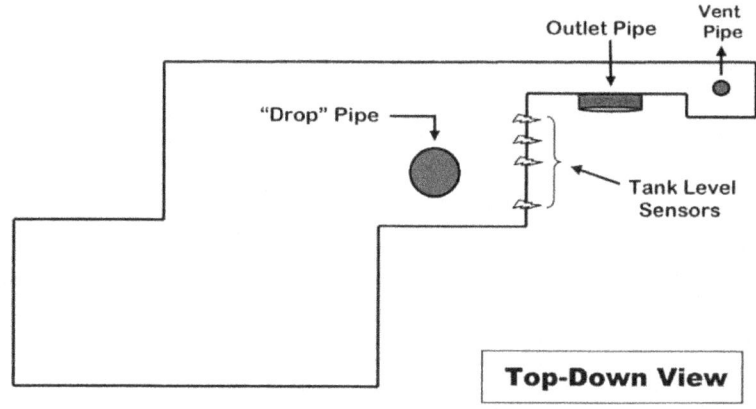

This leads us to two puzzling questions if you have one of these "flush" systems: **1.** "Where is the rinse nozzle oriented in relation to the 3" outlet pipe?" and **2.** "What kind of spray pattern does the rinse nozzle have?"

Here's a diagram of the most commonly encountered set-up:

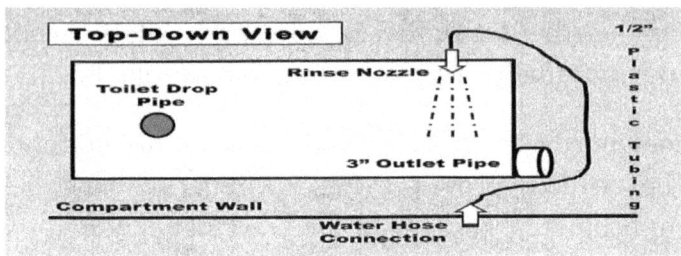

Any guesses how effective this arrangement is at rinsing the whole tank? And more challenging, if you have one, any idea how your rinse system is set up?

Not surprising at all, every OEM instructs all RV owners to "make sure the black valve is <u>open</u>" when rinsing a tank with a rinse system. That particular statement is more than likely an OEM legal caveat should the owner close the valve and inadvertently flood the coach's interior. (*BTW* – the flooding will show up either at the toilet or, if the toilet seals are really tight, at the rooftop opening of the tank vent.)

Many professional holding tank cleaners will readily recommend closing the black valve when using an installed rinsing system. This recommendation involves back-flooding the tank and using the previously mentioned hydrostatic head to remove more bio-waste from the tank (see page 36). This back-flooding is more effective than the OEM's instructed method. The difficulty is figuring out when the tank is full.

Caution: The previously mentioned Cardinal Rule about which hose to use with this system still applies (see page 38)!!

(Another *Very important Comment to consider:* The 1/2" clear plastic tubing from the Black Tank Flush system's water hose connection to the tank's rinse nozzle is pressure-sensitive [not reinforced] and could easily rupture/split if you fail to use a pressure regulator with your special [gray] "rinse" hose. [And I most definitely recommend a different (a.k.a. "rinsing") pressure regulator than the one you use for your freshwater hose, as well as **<u>NO</u>** water wyes in the flow path!])

Method #2: The Johnny Chock System

The 5" long, 2-3/8" diameter, fuchsia-colored Johnny Chock is a simple, hard, plastic tube with a 1/2" shoulder and two 1-1/2" grab tabs at one end (see page 48). To put this system to work, you merely open the toilet's flush valve and lower the chock into the opening – the shoulder is large enough that it won't fall through the flush valve's aperture. Because the flush valve is now blocked open, the water will automatically flow through the chock and into the black tank. The result is another type of back-flooding. To stop the process, simply remove the chock and let the flush valve close. You can use the aforementioned flashlight to monitor the water level in the tank by looking through the Johnny chock into the tank.

If this method seems to be a lot less complicated and safer than Method #1, that's only because it is!

How to make a rinsing method work efficiently for you

Note: Another rule-of-thumb – You are not ready to back-flood your black tank until you have the correct equipment.

If you plan to use the installed rinsing system (Method #1), invest in a 1/2" x 25' Gray Flushing Hose. This hose will match the inside diameter of your RV's plumbing. (Yes, that's important.) **Caution:** You need a "rinsing" pressure regulator at the bib.

If you plan to back-flood through the toilet (Method #2), invest in a Johnny Chock. **Caution:** You also need a pressure regulator at the bib.

Absolutely foremost, you must consistently use a pressure regulator at the water bib. You do not want the pressure of the water to be greater than **55** p.s.i. (see page 11)! This step applies to both Method #1 and #2. (**Remember:** Most RV plumbing systems typically have a "Do Not Exceed" pressure rating of sixty (**60**) p.s.i.)

SIGNIFICANT WARNING: Since safety and accuracy are of paramount importance, you <u>must</u> have the correct equipment and carefully observe all precautions associated with Back-Flooding! If you fail to comply and something "wrong" happens, <u>the onus is exclusively on **you**</u>!!

Calculating your Back-Flood Fill Time

While using a standard 40 to 50 p.s.i. pressure regulator at the bib for whichever method you choose, the flow rate into the black tank will be approximately 2.0 gallons per minute (g.p.m). The flow rate for the 50 to 55 p.s.i. (Hi-Flow) regulator is approximately 2.5 g.p.m. So…

The fill time for a 40-gallon holding tank @ 2.0 g.p.m. will be roughly 20 minutes. (40 gal ÷ 2.0 g.p.m. = 20 min.). And…

The fill time for a 40-gallon holding tank @ 2.5 g.p.m. will be roughly 16 minutes. (40 gal ÷ 2.5 g.p.m. = 16 min.).

<u>*Conclusion:*</u> A 40-gallon holding tank will require 16 to 20 minutes to fill completely, depending on which pressure regulator you use. *Note:* These same preliminary calculations <u>must</u> be made for the total gallon capacity of <u>your</u> RV's holding tank(s).

The Procedure's Initial Step(s)

If you use Method #1, attach your "rinsing" pressure regulator to the campground's water bib and the gray hose directly to the pressure regulator. Do <u>not</u> use a water wye at the bib when performing this back-flood procedure. A wye means there is another path for water to follow in addition to a path down the gray hose. Two paths open and running simultaneously, fed via the same bib, will result in lower than normal water pressure flowing down both paths, which <u>will</u> affect your tank fill timing.

Since most RVs don't have a shut-off valve at the toilet, you don't want water flowing into the toilet during the time you're connected to the rinse connection. Therefore, with a single flow path (e.g., bib » "rinsing" pressure regulator » gray hose » black tank rinse connection), make a note of the current time and open the bib valve to start the water flowing into the black tank.

If you are using Method #2, you will also have a single flow path (e.g., bib » pressure regulator » freshwater hose » RV's city water connection). However, since the water bib is already open, simply insert the Johnny Chock into the toilet's flush valve's opening to start the water flowing into the black tank, and make a note of the current time. Ensure that none of the sink faucets are opened to prevent a lower pressure during this back-flood procedure.

Verifying your Back-Flood Fill Time with Method #1

Unfortunately, with the black valve closed, there is no efficient way to tell just how full the Black Tank really is when using Method # 1. The tank level sensors may not have been installed with care and are essentially inaccurate. In the worst case, they are not functioning at all for some other reason(s). Guesswork, during this procedure, is neither the safe nor proficient way of doing things. Back-flooding requires 99.8% assurance.

Verifying your Back-Flood Fill Time with Method #2

With the previously calculated fill time for your black tank's capacity in mind, you will need to seriously start "babysitting" this procedure as soon as you start the water flowing into the tank. The best place to do this is, obviously, at the toilet. Start making regular visual checks of the water level in the tank with your "bathroom" flashlight. You will also need to listen closely to the sound of the water falling into the tank. (*Note:* If you have a double 45° "drop" pipe, listen very carefully!). There will be a distinct change in the pitch (it gets louder) when the water starts rising into the narrower "drop" pipe between the tank and the floor flange.

Once you've reached your calculated fill time, listen and check carefully to see if the tank is full. If it isn't, continue to <u>closely</u> monitor the filling process until the tank is full. When it is, stop the procedure. Make a note of the current time and calculate how long the fill genuinely took.

(*Comment:* You should perform the **Verifying Your Back-Flood Fill Time** procedure <u>several</u> <u>times</u> to ensure accuracy. Once tested and firmly established, the total fill time will remain nearly constant, **<u>as</u> <u>long</u> <u>as</u>** you religiously use the same type of pressure regulator when back-flooding.)

Follow-On Back-Flood Fills

After you have certified how long the "full" tank fill took, you can now calculate how long it will take to fill the tank to the "3/4 full" level. Multiply the total fill time by 0.75 (e.g. 20 minutes x 0.75 = 15 minutes). This will establish the amount of necessary time to back-flood the black tank to the all-important "3/4 full" level (and still leave you with a 1/4 of a tank safety factor).

The next time you execute/perform the procedure, the easiest way to monitor your fill time will be to use the timer on your smartphone or the RV's microwave. Set it for the "3/4 full" time (e.g., 15 minutes) and stop the procedure when the timer goes off. *WARNING:* It behooves you to stay <u>inside</u> the RV while the timer is running – you don't want to be somewhere else when it buzzes/dings. Your inattention could result in a disastrous event – flooding, flooding, flooding inside the RV living space! Of course, you can always use your "wait" time to browse the newspaper or read some more pages of your current book – just listen carefully for the applicable timer alert and respond accordingly.

Note: Utilizing either of the Back-Flood methods may take 2 or 3 fillings and drainings before you can see "successful" (a.k.a. "clear") rinsing results via your see-through hose adapter.

(*Comment:* During my seminars, I often refer to this adapter as being the original "RV TV." Once you start using one, you'll be watching it carefully whenever you drain the tanks. And, I've honestly witnessed several RVers pull up chairs and intently watch the tank contents flow by as they repeatedly fill and drain. Now, that's dedication to the process.)

(*Another Comment:* Here's an idea of how quickly your black tank will fill up under everyday use – with only two people in the RV, it will usually take between 6 to 8 days before a 40-gallon black tank needs to be drained [e.g. "3/4 full" or more]. And that includes the added "prepare" and "use" water.)

If you are traveling and want to drain and prepare the black tank every morning before hitting the road, the quickest and easiest method to use is Method #2 (The Johnny Chock Method). The back-flood fill time for "3/4 full" will still be germane – the amount of bio-waste the black tank collects in just one day is minimal, and you still have about a 1/4 of a tank safety factor.

(*Comment:* It's best to accomplish your back-flood and/or "prepare" procedure at a "full hookup" site and NOT at a "dump" station – please be considerate to the people in line behind you at the "dump" station.)

Adding the "Prepare" Water to an Empty Black Tank

You've already done the necessary total fill calculation. Now, all you have to do is multiply your total fill time by 0.25 (e.g., 20 minutes x 0.25 = 5 minutes). This establishes the necessary time to back-flood the black tank to the all-important "1/4 full" – Prepare level.

Other pieces of information to contemplate:

"Dump" is a euphemism for Drain.

You flush a toilet. You rinse a tank.

Rinsing is not Cleaning – it's just rinsing!

(It's nothing more than attempting to remove as much bio-waste as possible from the holding tank with a limited amount of water pressure.)

Pssst...
Here's another secret!

Rinsing alone will NOT remove a little known but <u>serious</u> holding tank problem!

STRUVITE

(*Comment:* This is mistakenly referred to as Mineral Build-Up – meaning it's believed to be hardened deposits of calcium carbonate or limestone from the water.)

Unless you work (or worked) in a municipal sewage treatment facility, you probably have never heard about this substance. However, it is actually a very prevalent problem in sewage and wastewater treatment facilities <u>worldwide</u>.

It was first identified in Hamburg, Germany, in 1845 by a geologist named Heinrich von Struve (hence, its name). He discovered that certain gases released from decomposing sewage react with an element in the water, bond together, and subsequently cause tanks and pipelines to be coated with cement-hard crystals (see Addendum # 5, page 79).

Struvite is a significant problem when anaerobic bacteria (the bad guys) control the quorum and release phosphate and ammonium while digesting the bio-waste material. Struvite crystals form whenever there is a 1:1:1 ratio of magnesium, phosphate, and ammonia in any holding tank. Magnesium is found in all the freshwater in the world. Phosphate is a dominant worldwide fertilizer found in our foods and the soaps and detergents we use. Ammonia comes from the breakdown of the urine in the wastewater.

(***Comment:*** Although it hasn't been proven yet, it's a plausible hypothesis that struvite starts to form immediately after the very first time we flush the toilet in a brand new RV.)

The most common locations for initial struvite formation and subsequent build-up are any points in the flow path that experience high turbulence. For example, in RVs, the struvite crystals build up on the inside structure of the toilet below the flush valve, on the exposed interior surface of the floor flange, on the piping leading in and out of the tank, in the corners, and on the walls of the tank, at the termination valve orifice when the blade is pulled open, and on the tank level sensors exposed to wastewater. In fact, struvite is the leading cause of black and gray holding tank sensor failures!

Struvite crystals are rough and porous, so they trap the unhealthy bio-solid waste (sludge) generated by the anaerobic, methane-forming bacteria in the tank. This thick sludge results in incomplete or slow drainage, as discussed earlier.

Here are some images that show what struvite looks like after it has been removed from an RV's holding tank

[Courtesy of Mr. Don Zimmerman, tanktechsrx.com]

Struvite "Chips" look like pieces of shale

[Courtesy of Mr. Don Zimmerman, tanktechsrx.com]

Struvite "Rocks" and "Sand"

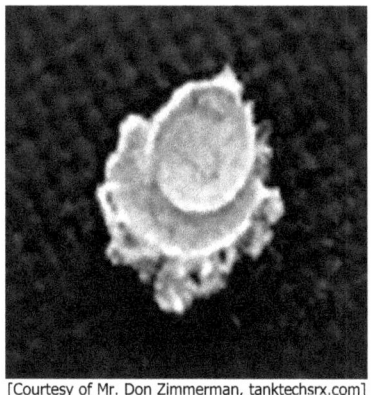

[Courtesy of Mr. Don Zimmerman, tanktechsrx.com]

A Struvite covered tank sensor

(Yes, that's correct – it is <u>not</u> toilet paper that prevents them from working!)

The First Visible Indication of Struvite Formation in your RV

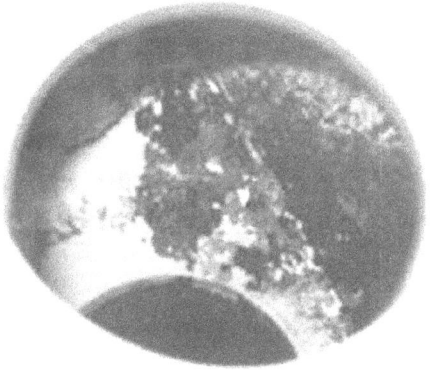

[Courtesy of Mr. Don Zimmerman, tanktechsrx.com]

Inside the toilet's throat – below the bowl, in between the ball/blade valve and the floor flange.

If you see it here, there's plenty more inside the tank!

What's the best way to "CLEAN" your holding tanks?

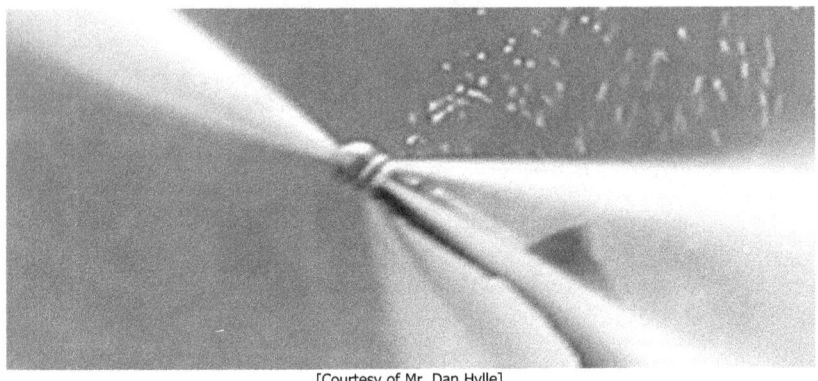

[Courtesy of Mr. Dan Hylle]

Professionally, with Hydro Jet Technology

The hydro-jet professionals use special nozzles with distinctive spray patterns (e.g., straight toward the front and angled toward the back) and high water pressure (around 3000 p.s.i.). This unique technology enables the high-pressure water to dislodge all bio-waste material(s) and struvite in the holding tank system – and, NO, it doesn't harm/damage your 3/8" to 1/4" thick-walled holding tanks. And, as a bonus feature, entry into the tanks is attained from the outside of the RV, at the termination valves – not from inside the RV. (*Comment:* Lower water pressure units [a.k.a., Electric Jetters/Pressure Washers that only operate between 800 to 1800 p.s.i.] cannot efficiently clean out a Pyramid Plug or rock hard Struvite.)

If you are using a chemical or enzyme tank treatment, how often should the holding tanks be cleaned?

    A. *Seasonal RV Use:* Before placing any RV into storage.

    B. *Long Term or Full-Time RV Use:* Annually (especially after extended-stay periods).

One Last Secret...

GRAY WATER IS NOT "JUST" WATER!

Your "Gray" tank contains many seemingly innocent, but actually jeopardous ingredients that you probably haven't thought about:

Soap, Toothpaste, Food Particles, Cooking Grease, Hair Follicles, Hair, Skin Cells, Saliva, and all sorts of Bacteria from your body.

Add these ingredients to a dark and moist environment, and you have the perfect breeding ground for:

* * *Mold & Disease* * *

Hmmm. Maybe it's a good idea to have your Gray holding tank professionally cleaned regularly as well!

And, oh yeah, draining the gray tank onto the ground is a malicious, anti-environmental act that you really **don't** want to commit. It's unlawful almost everywhere!

BTW – A probiotic, bio-waste treatment will kill mold and dissolve grease. It will also inhibit struvite formation and soften existing struvite so it can be hydro jetted out.

Caution: Using anti-bacterial soap(s) is counter-productive to using a probiotic treatment!

Rinsing the Gray Tank
(a.k.a. "Flushing")

This is one task that most RVers don't even think of. And, yes, I confess, until I had my tanks cleaned for the first time in October of 2007 (see In Memoriam on page 3), I had never considered rinsing my gray tank. In fact, I hadn't even realized it might be necessary. As I think back on it, I don't remember anyone mentioning anything about rinsing out a gray tank!

I wondered if a Gray Tank Flush system (similar to the Black Tank Flush system) existed. So I checked with sales and tech friends at many large RV dealerships around the country to see if any of them had seen or heard of such a thing. But, unfortunately, at that time, I didn't find anyone who had.

While pondering about how to possibly rinse out the gray tank, it dawned on me just how easily it could be done without special equipment. So here's what I came up with:

1. The bathroom sink drains directly into the gray tank. If I turn the cold-water faucet <u>fully/wide</u> <u>open</u>, the water will controllably flow into the sink and then into the gray tank.

2. Because the tub/shower pan has the lowest plumbing drain inside any RV, I actually have a tell-tale location for identifying when the gray tank is full!

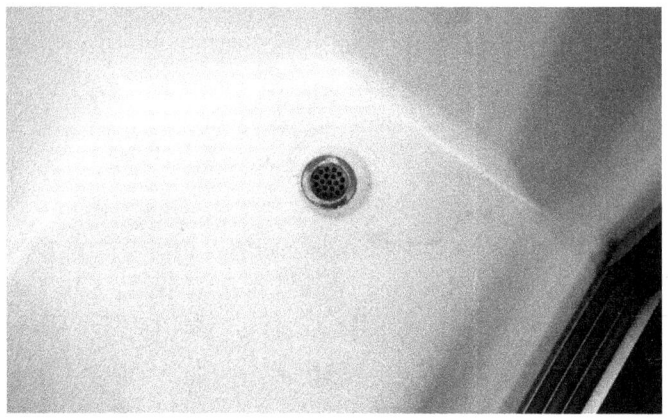

3. End result: As soon as the water starts to backflow into the tub/shower pan, the gray tank is obviously full and over-filling. TO STOP THE BACKUP, all I have to do is "close" the cold-water faucet at the sink.

Since I always use a 40 to 50 p.s.i. pressure regulator at the water bib, I knew the water flow rate at the sink would be the same as the water flow rate at the toilet (yes, I use the Johnny Chock System). So I next proceeded to drain the gray tank and start my time test to see how long it would take for the gray tank to fill (see page 52).

And…, violà! – 20 minutes to fill; that verified I had a 40-gallon gray tank! Back-flooding and rinsing the gray tank will be just as easy as the black tank via the toilet.

p.s. Anyone with an additional "kitchen/galley" gray tank (as in some 5th wheels) could use this same concept to back-flood and rinse that extra tank.

NOTE: All the *WARNINGS* applying to back-flooding the black tank also apply to the gray tank!

A recommendation – re: your Gray tank

Gray tank odors have ruined more RVing activities than the black tanks ever will. In fact, the most frequent source of offensive odor in an RV is actually the galley/gray tank. In addition, gray tanks are the perfect environment for mold growth and E. coli bacteria.

Besides venting through the roof, Gray tanks are also vented under the sink with a special "check vent" (actually designated as an Anti-Siphon Trap Vent Device [ASTVD]) to prevent tank gases from entering the RV. However, nothing stops the gases from entering the coach through <u>dry, or nearly dry</u>, sink or shower p-traps. You just don't realize how quickly the liquid in a p-trap will spill out as any RV bounces and rocks down the road. The industry recognizes this issue and is experimenting with new, collapsible sink traps to stop the odor backflow. (Hep_vO is one brand name [see Addendum # 2, page 75].)

These odors are very offensive and annoying. For this reason, it is recommended that gray tanks be treated with a probiotic, especially in motorhomes, before traveling. An open window can pull the gases out of the tank via a dry/nearly dry p-trap, filling the coach as they move toward the open window (it's called a venturi effect).

Therefore…, even if you leave your galley tank open while staying at a site with full hookups, **always travel with enough water in the gray tank to keep the bottom wet.** ("Prepare" it just like the black tank – add water by opening the cold-water faucet at the bathroom sink and timing the flow.) Adding a probiotic treatment to the tank will combat the mold and odors. It will also clean as you go, keep you safe, and get the tank ready for the next stop!

One last remark about your Gray tank

You've already learned that it's not a good idea to leave your black tank valve open. But, what about the gray tank valve. Open or Closed? There has been a great deal of controversy about this one:

1. Some people say, "Keep it closed, except when draining the tank. If you leave it open, you are just inviting sewer gas and "critters" from the campground's sewer system into your RV.

Who knows what can crawl into the Gray tank!"

[Courtesy of Mr. Dan Hylle]

(*Comments:* **a**. The most common "critters" that enter your RV via the gray tank appear to be large fruit flies. However, they are tiny flies often referred to as sink flies, drain flies, sewer flies, or sewer gnats. They are harmless; they do not transmit human diseases, nor do they bite. However, they can cause contamination of food because they come from a seriously unhygienic source.

b. And, they are absolutely infuriating when they're flying around. They typically have a one to three-week life cycle and are very difficult to kill with the usual chemical sprays [although a fly swatter seems to work very well]. If you use a probiotic tank treatment, the aerobic bacteria will attack any "sewer fly" eggs and larvae they can find and, thus, prevent any new adults from appearing to replace the ones you swatted.)

2. Yet, other people, especially those who occupy their RVs for extended stays, say, "If I leave the valve closed, it seems like I'm emptying the gray tank every other day. I like the convenience of being able to use the sinks and shower freely, without worrying about filling the gray tank."

Well, folks, there is a quick answer to this dilemma. Just install a p-trap in your sewer hose. It's so simple. The picture below describes it best:

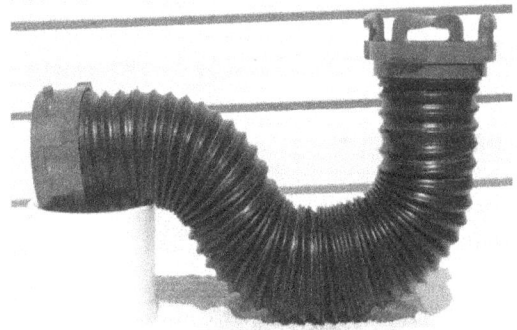

Now your sewer hose will function just like the piping under your sinks and tub/shower. This "p-trap" keeps out the campground's sewer gas and most of the obnoxious "critters" but still allows the gray water to escape freely. (**Warning:** You must remove the p-trap before draining and rinsing the black tank. This p-trap will slow the black tank's bio-waste and wastewater movement, thus causing inefficient drainage.)

A permanent fix would require installing electric dump valves. (**Comment:** I've tried them all and prefer the EZ-Valve manufactured by Valterra. They have the best "fail-safe," manually activated, backup dump capability. **p.s.** I installed the gray switch in the bathroom – that way, it was easy to reach [and dump] if the gray tank overfilled while either of us were in the shower.)

In Review

There are six (6) necessary steps to ensure appropriately functioning RV bio-waste holding tanks

1. **Prepare** – Always fill empty "Black" and "Gray" tanks with water to "1/4 full" level (e.g., 10 gallons of water to a 40-gallon tank).

2. **Treat** – Use a Probiotic Tank Treatment. (Do **NOT** combine with any other tank treatments or chemicals.)

3. **Use** – Pre-fill toilet bowl "1/2 or 3/4 full" before use. (Water-Water-Water!)

4. **Drain** – Do NOT "dump" the "Black" holding tank until "3/4 or almost full." Drain the Black tank first and the Gray tank second. Never have both valves open at the same time.

5. **Rinse** – Back-Flood Rinse with the installed Tank Rinsing System or with a Johnny Chock.
   Warning: You MUST monitor either operation closely!

6. **Clean** – Professional Hydro Jet Cleaning (High Pressure cleaning – around **3000** p.s.i.) When?
   - A. *Seasonal RV Use:* Before placing any RV into storage.
   - B. *Long Term or Full-Time RV Use:* Annually (especially after extended-stay periods).

Some Final Remarks About Tank Cleaning

With the regular use of probiotics in your holding tanks, it may not be necessary to have your tanks cleaned every year – maybe every second or third year!

In addition, if your RV is routinely stored in a non-freezing part of the country during the "off" season, a probiotic treatment can be added to a holding tank and then filled with water. The aerobic bacteria will be working to clean the holding tank(s) until everything is gone!

Of course, suppose you are still using a chemical or enzyme treatment. In that case, it is undoubtedly a good idea to have your tanks cleaned annually.

And, with that, I think we can safely wrap up this overview of your RV's most mysterious secrets and unpleasant chores.

Hopefully, this book has caused you to view RV bio-waste management differently and realize that your proactive participation is essential to obtaining and maintaining healthy and happy, "temporary" holding tanks.

Thank you for reading this *Primer*.

May you always use the "right" tools when you are draining and rinsing your RV's holding tanks.

Sincerely,

Dale

www.sumdalus.com

Closing Notes

TankTechsRx

Where can you get it?

If your local RV dealership or supplier doesn't carry TankTechsRx, you can always acquire it online from the manufacturer at *JustScience.com*.

It is sold in 16 oz and 32 oz bottles.

Manufacturer's Suggested Retail Price

16 oz bottle (up to 32 tank treatments) - $29.95.
32 oz (up to 64 tank treatments) - $44.95.

For price comparisons, you can always check Amazon.com.

Looking for "How-To" videos?

Head to the TankTechsRx YouTube channel for many instructional videos, testimonials and much more.

https://www.youtube.com/user/TanktechsRx

Have a really stubborn Black Tank problem? Feel free to contact *Just Science* at 1-800-625-7945 and ask for Don.

Index

Topics

Topic	Page
Addendum # 1 – "Cleaning the Toilet"	74
Addendum # 2 – "Hep$_V$O Sanitary Waste Valve"	75
Addendum # 3 – "Water Adhesion"	76
Addendum # 4 – "Dumping in Ten (10) Easy Steps"	78
Addendum # 5 – "More About Struvite"	79
Addendum # 6 – "Using Probiotics While Traveling"	80
Bacteria Based Treatment	28
Belly Bulge	46
Black Tank Rinsing System	49
Chemical Based Treatment	26
Drop Type?	20
Enzyme Based Treatment	27
Formaldehyde Based Treatment	25
Gray Tank Info	61
House Plumbing System	9
Introduction	6
Johnny Chock System	51
Probiotics	33
RV Plumbing System	11
Six (6) Necessary Steps to Healthy Holding Tanks	15
Step One – Prepare	16
Step Two – Treat	24
Step Three – Use	17

Topics (cont'd)

	Page
Step Four – Drain	45
Step Five – Rinse	48 & 62
Step Six – Clean	60
Struvite	56
Toilet Paper	23
Use the RIGHT Tools	38
Using the WRONG Tools	43

Diagrams

	Page
5th Wheel Trailer – Not Enough Water	19
Acid Forming Bacteria	31
Gray Tank P-Trap	66
Hydrostatic Head	36
Motorhome/Trailer – Not Enough Water	18
Bio-waste digester bacteria	32

ADDENDUM # 1
(August 7, 2015)

"How do I clean the toilet bowl when using a probiotic?" is the most frequent question I receive during the seminars I present about holding tanks.

There are indeed two products you **don't** want to use: Bleach and/or the usual "Cleaning" Chemicals. Both are biocides and will kill all the desired "good" bacteria, as well as the "bad."

My wife has gone back to using what her grandmother had used to clean the bathroom. White Vinegar!

Yes, the simple, distilled white vinegar. Admittedly, it is a mild acid (about 5% acetic acid) but is well recognized as a cleaning agent. It is especially effective in removing inorganic soils, organic waste, and mineral deposits such as hard water films."

(***Comment:*** The following procedures occur just before "dumping" our holding tanks. First, my wife uses a spray bottle filled with undiluted white vinegar to clean our toilet, sinks, and shower stall. Then, protected by disposable gloves, she sprays the vinegar onto the "dirty" surfaces and wipes them down with paper towels. Next, the paper towels and gloves are disposed of in a trash container and, then the "cleaned" surfaces are thoroughly rinsed with freshwater. After she has finished, I get the signal to "drain and back-flood" the holding tanks. Easy-Peasy.

All things considered, the "3/4 full" prep of the bowl [which also reduces the occurrence of "skid marks" in the bowl], combined with the use of white vinegar as a cleaning agent, leaves us with a "sanitary and fresh" toilet without killing our hard-working, "good," decomposing bacteria. A win-win situation, for sure.)

ADDENDUM # 2
(July 26, 2016)

For more information about the Hep$_v$O Sanitary Waste Valve and how it can help eliminate obnoxious sewer odors in an RV, please check out the following YouTube video from the RV Doctor, Gary Bunzer.

www.youtube.com/watch?v=2QV6drbFbK0
(Case specific & the last character is a numeric ZERO, not a capital O.)

As an added bonus, you'll be surprised at how easily they are to install, as well as how much storage space you can add under the sinks by installing a Hep$_v$O valve (e.g., in the image below, the upper shelf would have been virtually unusable with a P-trap in place).

Another bonus – no need to put RV antifreeze down the drains when winterizing.

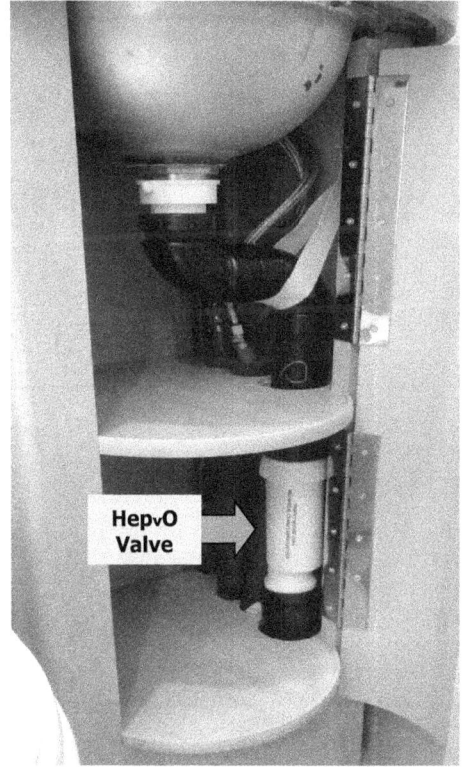

[Courtesy of Mr. Gary Bunzer, rvdoctor.com]

ADDENDUM # 3
(July 16, 2017)

Draining your black tank is not a case of the bio-waste "floating" out of a black tank or being "pushed" out by the flow of the water. It is actually a case of the water "pulling" the bio-waste out of our black tank as it flows out. This "pulling" effect is the result of a phenomenon called Water Adhesion. Water adhesion refers to the attraction of water to other surfaces. You've seen it many times before. Here's just one example: (Adhesion causes water to "stick" to Pine Needles after a rain.)

[Source: J. Schmidt; National Park Service]
(Modified by Author)

In our black holding tank, it is metaphorically like this:

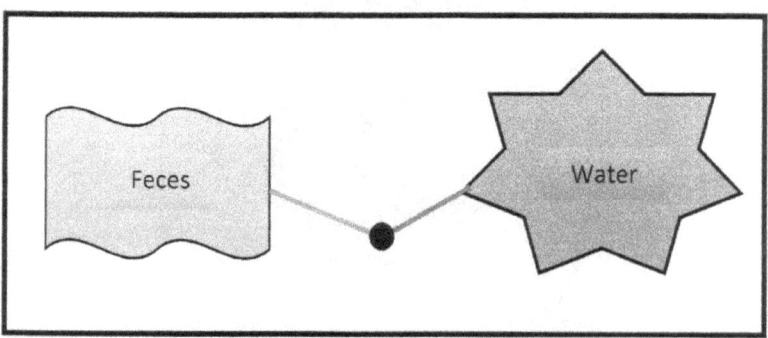

Natural Water Adhesion

However, whenever a "Surfactant" is added to a holding tank as an ingredient in any type of "treatment," the adhesion bond will be broken. A surfactant is a compound that significantly lowers the surface tension between water and the bio-wastes in your black tank. Without this surface tension, the water can no longer adhere to the bio-waste and "pull" it along.

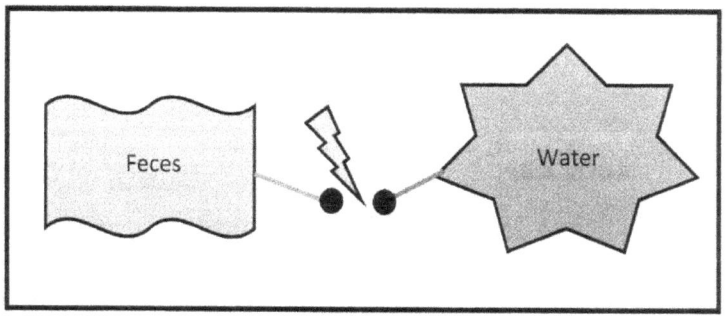

Addition of a Surfactant

(**Comment:** It certainly behooves you to carefully read all of the label information on any holding tank treatment you are contemplating using.)

ADDENDUM # 4
(July 16, 2017)

10 Easy Steps to Safe and Successful Holding Tank "Dumping."

Step 1. Tools (see pages 38 through 42).

Step 2. Gloves (see pages 38, 43, and 44).

Step 3. Hose Adapter (see page 39).

Step 4. Extension Hose(s)," Drop" Coupler, and Support System (see pages 40 and 41).

Step 5. Gray Valve (see page 45).

Step 6. Draining (see pages 36 and 37, plus pages 45 through 47).

Step 7. Rinsing (see pages 48 through 56).

Step 8. Treat (see pages 24 through 35).

Step 9. Prepare (see pages 16 through 19).

Step 10. Clean-Up (see page 42).

ADDENDUM # 5
(July 16, 2017)

More About Struvite

Source: jenfitch.com]

This image shows just how badly struvite can actually block the smooth passage of waste and fluids. This struvite choked pipe is from a fourteen (14) inch diameter line at a municipal treatment facility. It usually allows sludge to transfer from an anaerobic digester to a sludge holding pond/tank.

Imagine what it can do to your RV's much smaller holding tank system!

ADDENDUM # 6
(July 16, 2017 – updated June 5, 2021)

Using a Probiotic Treatment While Traveling

TankTechsRx's product labeling recommends not fully draining and flushing your holding tanks. Instead, they recommend draining until the flow rate subsides, then close the valve to retain some water and some of the existing "live mother culture" (a.k.a. aerobic bacteria). Additionally, they recommend waiting until your holding tanks are "full" before draining them.

Although we find this to be very sound advice while we are "planted" in one spot for any period of time, we have adopted a variance to their recommendation – primarily when we travel with our RV.

As previously stated on page 13 of this *Primer*, water weighs 8.34 pounds per gallon. If you have 40-gallon holding tanks (black & gray), and if both tanks are between 1/2 capacity to full, that means the contents of each tank will weigh between 167 and 334 pounds. Double those numbers, and you have between 334 and 668 pounds total weight of wastewater you're carrying around. Add that to the weight of any freshwater you are carrying (our FW tank holds 75 gals or 626 pounds of water), and you are hauling around some seriously unnecessary weight. (*Comment:* Admittedly, where we live in middle Georgia, fuel is currently around $2.69 to $2.99 per gallon and not over $4.00 per gallon as it once was (it was only $1.35 per gallon when my wife and I started full-timing in 2002). Nevertheless, do you really want to pay the additional fuel expense to haul around all that water weight?

So, here's what we do when traveling with our RV. First, as explained on page 13, we always travel with our freshwater tank empty. There are plenty of water/beverage sources available along the way. Second, we always drain, rinse, and "prepare" our tanks before starting out on the road. We travel until we reach our first night's layover campground. After the morning rituals (breakfast, shower, teeth, etc.), we use the Johnny Chock method (see page 51) to fill our black tank to its 3/4 full level and the bathroom sink method (see pages 62 and 63) to fill the gray tank about the same. Then, we drain the black tank completely and back-flood to 3/4 full once. After the rinse is completed, we treat with our usual 1/2 ounce of probiotic and "prepare" with a 1/4 fill. After the black tank is completed, we start draining the gray tank. When the flow has diminished to a small rivulet (no longer a flood flow), we do, indeed, close the gray valve to trap some water and some of the mother culture. However, we only pour 1/4 ounce of probiotic down the bathroom sink when treating the gray tank and "prepare" with only a 1/8 fill. (*Comment:* We do this gray tank routine even when we are "planted." That's because, like everyone else's, our gray tank fills up every 2 to 2-1/2 days. Hence, it is drained 2 or 3 times more often than the black tank.)

We perform this ritual every morning before hitting the road. The black tank is drained "completely" because it only receives a minimum of daily and evening deposits. The gray tank is drained "partially" because it receives more water deposits than the black tank (showers and dishwashing). Each tank will have almost a full 24-hour period (see page 30 for bacteria growth rate – and that's starting with just for one (1) bacterium) to rebuild its live mother culture before the process is repeated the following day of travel. Once we reach our destination, we'll continue to capture deposits in both tanks until they are nearly full.

We believe this variance allows us to travel with minimal extra water weight, and we can still maintain a positive probiotic system.

About Dale, the RV Tech, Teacher, & Author . . .

Dale Lee Sumner is a retired RVIA/RVDA Master Certified RV Service Technician and former owner/president of Mobile RV Medic, Inc.

He has sixty years of experience using and living in RVs (including more than a decade of recent "full-time" RVing) and conducting the business of repairing RVs. Now, he is concentrating on educating the RV owners.

And...Dale loves to teach what he writes! His goal is to provide as many RVers as possible – be they initially "Considering" RVing, just "Beginning" to RV, been "Camping" for years, or are living the dream of "Full-Timing" – with a solid, baseline understanding of the different (non-house-like) functional areas in their RVs.

Dale's teaching style is educational yet casual and entertaining. He writes in a down-to-earth, non-technical fashion so every reader can quickly become familiar with the subject(s).

I sincerely hope you enjoyed this book. If you did, please comment about it on social media and, surely, write an Amazon or Goodreads review.

And, of course, please tell a friend about this book – especially if your friend owns an RV or is thinking about getting one.

Thank you for your support,

Dale Lee Sumner

p.s. You may want to check out the **RV Blog** page on our website: sumdalus.com

www.ingramcontent.com/pod-product-compliance
Lightning Source LLC
Chambersburg PA
CBHW060416050426
42449CB00009B/1990